Fireflies at Midnight

To Laura, Hiro, and Kento—M. S.
For Maria—K. R.

Atheneum Books for Young Readers
An imprint of Simon & Schuster Children's Publishing Division
1230 Avenue of the Americas
New York, New York 10020

Book design by Sonia Chaghatzbanian
The text of this book is set in Goudy.
The illustrations are rendered as photographic treatments.

Printed in Hong Kong
First Edition

10 9 8 7 6 5 4 3 2 1

Library of Congress Cataloging-in-Publication Data
Singer, Marilyn.
Fireflies at midnight / by Marilyn Singer ; pictures by Ken Robbins.
p.   cm.
ISBN 0-689-82492-0
1. Insects—Juvenile poetry. 2. Animals—Juvenile poetry. 3. Children's poetry, American.
[1. Insects—Poetry. 2. Animals—Poetry. 3. American poetry.]
I. Robbins, Ken, ill. II. Title.
PS3569.I546 F57 2002
811(.54—dc21   00-054282

Fireflies at Midnight

BY Marilyn Singer   PICTURES BY Ken Robbins

Atheneum Books for Young Readers
New York London Toronto Sydney Singapore

robin

Up cheerup I'm up
Let me be first to greet the light
First cheerily first
Hello day, good-bye night

Up cheerup I'm up
In this tree soon chicks will hatch
Soon cheerily soon
Down below are worms to catch

Up cheerup I'm up
Hail chicks and worms and sky!
Hail cheerily hail
Morning robins are not shy

otter

It starts with the slide
   with the mud
   with the ride
Then the splash
   and the dip
   and the flip
and the glide
Next the catch-a-quick
   munch
or the leisurely lunch
It's the tussle with the mussel
   or the clever crayfish crunch
Then the float
   and the cruise
   and the lull

and the snooze
Or the snuggle
   and the nestle
Before the wake-up
   and the wrestle
or the race
and the chase
It's the pond
   that's the place
where we play
   every day
the brand-new
   and the same
wet and welcome
   otter game

Crayfish

I, crayfish,
   no day fish
   no way fish
at all
Nosy otter, watch its jaws
Careless wader, watch my claws
Spend each morning
   lying soundless
     under stones
Spend each evening
   shredding stems
     picking bones

 Horse

Early morning,
Early evening is a nice time
    to canter
a nifty time
    to trot
But not noon
    in July or June
It's too hot
Better then to stand
    naked—
no saddle
no bridle—
    nibbling grass
under the everyday sun
rather than get in a lather
Let chipmunks chase
    piglets race
and ninny dogs
    run

Ants

One and one and one and one
    Dead leaves
    Dead crickets
One ant alone can't pick it
    up
can't drag this meal to our busy nest
But one and one and one and one
    Together we tow
    Together we know
any time of day this is so:
One and one and one and one
    is the best way
    to get things done

Monarch Butterfly

Wait I can wait
    For the fullness of wings
    For the lift   For the flight
Wait I can wait
    A moment less
    A moment more
I have waited much longer before
    For the taste of the flower
    For the feel   For the sight
Wait I can wait
    For the prize of the skies
    For the gift of the air
Almost finished
Almost there
    Almost ready
        to rise

Red Eft

There is a pond
    waiting
There is a road
    crossing
There are rocks
    blocking
       logs and leaf litter
    lying
       in the way
The way before the road
    crossing
       the pond
    waiting
But after all the afternoon
    is long
       and warm
And I have four steady legs
       few enemies
and all the time
       in the world

Rabbit

watch me
     don't watch me
don't see me
     in the grass
pass me by
I'm a trick of the eye
don't chase
     just erase
what you see
one small smudge
     that won't budge
it's not me

Bat

I hear/I see
   the night
come creeping in
I hear/I see
   a cousin
flutter by
I hear/I see
   the trees
rise in my path
I hear/I see
   a house
where days I sleep
I hear/I see
   in waves of sound
Mosquitoes swarm
I ride a breeze
The air is warm
I hear/I see
I fly   I find
I near
   I seize

Frog

baron I'm the baron
I'm the duke
I'm the king
    of this piece of the pond
when it's muggy
when it's buggy
    in the moonlight
hear me sing
baron I'm the baron
I'm the duke
I'm the king

Firefly

Come
   (flash)
Choose me
   (flash flash)
I am the
   (flash)
summer romancer
In the night
   (flash)
My light
   (flash)
asks Are You The One?
Come
   (flash)
flash me back
   the answer

Red Fox

These summer nights I—
    always the hunter—
will lead them
    where the blueberries are sweetest
    where the crunchy crickets hatch
and maybe—
      if they are ready—
    where to snare a frog
        or two
These summer nights I—
    always the hunter—
will teach them
    how to spot the turtle's tasty eggs
    how to hear the beetles buried in the grass
and maybe—
      if they are ready—
    how to catch a vole
        or two
These summer nights I—
    sometimes the mother—
will show my bouncing pouncing pups
    why no one ever mocks
      a fox

Spider

Web is the work
    is the home
    is the trap
    is the hub
    is the map
    is the night
    is the day
    is the hour
    is the power
    is the pattern
is the way

In the beneath
    it is mole time
    the whole time
Curl up and sleep
    Sleep so deep
            down
      below
    Sleep for hours
      safe and still
Be a loafer not a gopher
Digging's best
But Mole needs rest

Sleep unhurried
    Sleep unworried
Dream of grubs
    by the number
If Earth shakes

Mole awakes
But soil just sifting
means time for drifting
    Welcome slumber